The Roy Greavesly Letters

Cover Design by Rob Cureton, Orful Comics
www.orfulcomics.co.uk.

Computer wizardry by Martin Nicholson.

ISBN-13 978-1491016879
ISBN-10-1491016876

First published 2013.

Dedication

For Dec Munro, legendary purveyor of 'Test Tube Comedy.'

Roy Greavesley

15/07/08

Dear Roy

I was passed your letter by our editor ████████. I was very interested in your story, especially the custard incident. I have to say I don't quite believe it but I'm happy to be proven wrong. Can you contact me with your telephone number. My contact details are above.

Cheers

Tom

Dramatic Prologue

I was standing next to a drum kit on Christmas Day 1997 when I told my wife Karen I'd been having an affair and was leaving her. As the shock on her face began to register I quickly tapped out the drumbeat from the *Eastenders* credits. Karen immediately got the joke and we laughed until we cried. Over the next few years it became tradition for me to make the same announcement, each time on Christmas morning, always careful to make sure I was standing next to a drum kit. Then, one morning in 2007, Karen told me she'd been having an affair with 'Gary,' a tattooed, thirty-two year old electrician. I looked around in vain, but she wasn't standing anywhere near a drum kit. If you yourself have a drum kit, you may wish to make use of it now.

One month later, after drinking an enormous volume of alcohol and reading a library of self-help books, I drove to Karen's new home to try and win her back. Gary hovered menacingly in the background as I asked Karen to reconsider. Her reply was chilling. *"Go away Roy or you will force my new boyfriend to be unnecessarily violent and aggressive."*

Back home I cried real tears and sought support from friends, even throwing up over myself during a coffee with my friend Nev. Recipients of my nightly calls were initially supportive. But after three weeks of listening to my pain and woe they began avoiding them, Nev even going so far as to fake his own death and stage a bogus funeral attended by some three hundred people at great time and expense.

I fell into depression. I drank heavily. I refused to go into work until finally I was sacked.

I had no job. No wife. Reality was too painful. So one night, drunk, lonely, delusional and confused, I began writing some letters. For some time I was unable to stop.

Please note: I have protected the identities of the individuals and companies who were kind enough to respond to me throughout what was a very difficult time. Each and every letter however is COMPLETELY REAL. Add another dramatic drumbeat here if you wish.

To A Well Known Confectioner

Monday 12th November 2007

Dear Sir or Madam,

I write to you sincerely in the hope that you can be of assistance in this matter. I am currently separated from my wife by the M6 and she has initiated divorce proceedings. I have been devastated by this, even more so by details that have come to light regarding her ongoing affair with Gary, a tattooed, thirty-two year old electrician.

After eleven (I thought) happy years, I not only face the awful truth that my marriage is over, but am also battling alone against my wife and her new partner's demands.

I will admit that I am angry at the prospect of having to give her half of everything I own and wish to send a symbolic message that I will no longer be pushed around.

As my (soon to be ex) wife loves your products I wish to request if you can make an exact replica of my head from chocolate? My wife would no doubt place this object on her mantlepiece and the subliminal message that I am watching her would be more effective than a forthright letter from my solicitor who, judging by the sums of money I may have to hand over, is both ineffective and inept.

To enhance the effect I would like the face to display a tremendously frightening scowl that clearly delineates my disapproval.

I thank you for taking time to evaluate this sincere request. Naturally I would be happy to cover the necessary costs and would submit to a mould being made of my head.

I am, yours most sincerely

Roy Greavesly

17 December 2007

Mr R Greavesley

Dear Mr Greavesley,

Thank you for your recent letter from which we were most concerned to learn of the difficult time you are experiencing.

Whilst we fully sympathise with the situation you find yourself in, it is with regret that we are unable to assist with your request.

Please accept our sincere apologies for being unable to progress your request further on this occasion. We do hope that the start of next year will be a little easier for you.

Thank you for contacting us and we would like to wish you a Merry Christmas from all at ▋▋▋▋

Yours sincerely

Consumer Relations Department

18th December 2007

Dear Karen,

Thankyou for your recent letter in which you stated that you are never coming back.

I hope that we can remain civil. With this in mind, would it be possible to meet with you once a week and have sexual intercourse?

Forever.

Roy

To A Reputable Hotel.

4th January 2008

Dear Sir or Madam,

I am seeking to create a very special event for my wife on our wedding anniversary and your hotel would be my first choice to host this.

I would like to book a surprise evening for my wife that takes a James Bond theme. The aim would be to re-create three scenes from my wife's favourite Bond film – 'Moonraker' featuring Roger Moore and femme fetale Corrinne Dufour.

This would necessitate our use of a suitable place to accomodate our arrival by helicopter (I will hire an accomplished pilot.) I would also require a high ceilinged drawing room with one grand piano (to be played by an actor hired to capture the dangerous essence of Bond villain Hugo Drax) and one large bedroom, where, needing information, I would seduce an (at first) unwilling 'Corrinne.'

The next morning I would like to particpate in a duck shoot with a brooding Drax, shortly after which 'Corrinne' is chased into the woods by two doberman pinscher's. This would then end our re-enactment and we would like to return to the hotel for refreshment before leaving for home.

I would greatly appreciate an appreciation of the cost implications for my proposed event and hope you feel able to accomodate it.

Yours most sincerely

Roy Greavesly

Mr Roy Greavesly

7th January 2008

Dear Mr Greavesly

Many thanks for enquiry received 3rd January 2008. We are delighted that you are considering █████ for your special event.

Without a date for your anniversary it is a little difficult to provide you with a full proposal for your event, however I have I looked into each request and we are able to offer the following, subject to availability:

- Arrival by helicopter – This would be no problem subject to an authorisation form being signed in advance.
- Drawing Room – We have 21 function rooms here at █████ and a number of these could be themed as a drawing room. It would be wise for you to come in to see these rooms to decide which would be most appropriate. The room hire would be between £300 and £2000.00 depending on your preferred choice of room.
- Dinner, bed and breakfast – Again, this is no problem and the rate will depend on when you choose to hold the event.

We have had a little more difficulty in finding a solution to some of the requests, so we have requested the assistance of one our partners companies, █████. They have provided a quote for Clay Pigeon Shooting (duck shooting cannot be offered) and also a Grand Piano and Pianist (quotes enclosed) but we are still at a loss with regards to the 2 dobermen and a Hugo Drax lookalike.

If you would like further details, please do not hesitate to contact me with an idea of the dates that you would consider. If you could provide me with a telephone number, I would be happy to call you to discuss the event in greater detail.

Kindest regards

Friday 11th January 2008

Dear Kelly,

I must thankyou for your letter dated 7th January regarding my proposed event. The pricing seems most reasonable and I am happy with the clay pigeon shooting option. The remaining obstacles I think we agree are the doberman's and the question of Drax.

Perhaps the pianist himself could be Drax? My only reservation would be whether he would be brooding enough. Drax is a supervillian hell bent on creating his own master race in a space station after destroying all human life on earth. Such ambitions must weigh heavy. Drax must have a certain economy of movement to be convincing. He must convey a strong sense of purpose with an effortless calm, but beneath this veneer there must a rage. Simmering.

With regards the doberman's I now feel confident I could supply them myself. There are however two other matters which I neglected to mention through error, but which must be included in the experience.

I would like Drax to have a henchman called 'Cha.' He should be of Chinese extraction and wear a small bowl haircut and moustache.

After the meeting in the drawing room, Drax must instruct Cha to kill me. I would therefore like Cha to attack me in the hotel grounds after dinner with a kendo pole.

I thought initially I might rehearse the fight with Cha but on reflection feel this would be more exciting *sans le choreograph.* The experience must smack of danger as my wife says I haven't done anything dangerous in years.

With this in mind there is also the issue of Jaws. If possible I would like a seven foot giant with metal teeth hiding in the wardrobe when we arrive in our room. Jaws would not need to try and kill me, his role would simply be to scare the hell out of my wife.

Do forgive me for replying in writing – my wife closely monitors the phone and I do not dare risk spoiling the surprise. Anyhow, I must grow accustomed to doing things in secret!

The details are important – I am happy to visit the hotel and watch 'Moonraker' with you in full if that will help. Our anniversary is June 7th and time is running close.

Yours most sincerely

Roy Greavesly

21 January 2008

Mr Roy Greavesly
██████████████████████

Dear Mr Greavesly

██

Thank you for your second letter dated 11th January 2008.

Further to your letter I have spoken with Nick at ████████████ and he is confident that his pianist, ████████████ will be brooding enough for you! Although not a Drax lookalike, should you wish to proceed with the booking they would be happy to look into a suitable costume for him to wear.

Again, we are struggling to find a Cha lookalike, however ████████████ have sourced a Jaws lookalike. I have enclosed their proposal for this.

I am due to go on ████████ leave from Friday 25th January 2008 therefore any further correspondence should be sent for the attention of my colleague, ████████████, Special Events Manager who will be happy to help in my absence.

I do feel that it would be of huge benefit for you to visit ████████ to discuss your event with Jill and Nick from ████████ During your visit we would be happy to show you the choice of function rooms, bedrooms and also the grounds in which your activities could take place. Please contact Jill to arrange a convenient time. In the meantime, I have enclosed a proposal based on the details we have been successful in arranging so far.

Kindest regards

To A City Council

Monday 14th January 2008

Good Morning,

I am writing to ask if you have any objection to me being Roger Moore for a day?

On March 16th I would like to walk about the city in a flared trouser suit, raising my eyebrow at whosoever I wish.

Naturally during the course of the day several people will try to kill me. Naturally I will defeat them with ungainly martial arts moves after initially allowing them the upper hand.

I intend to take a room at a reputable hotel and seduce a total of four women. Initially of course they will be reluctant, but all barriers shall melt with my 'sucking poison from a wound' kissing technique.

Do you have any objection to me being Moore? I admire his portrayal of The Great Secret Agent and would like to continue my preparations without delay.

Yours most sincerely

Roy Greavesly

Mr Roy Greavesly

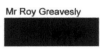

Dear Mr Greavesly

Thank you for your letter dated 14th January 2008.

 City Council has no objections to your request provided that you stay within the law.

Yours sincerely,

Festivals & Events Assistant

cc. ▮▮▮▮▮▮▮▮   Chief Executive

To A Well Known Brewery

VELVET SKY FILM

Thursday 27th December 2007

Dear Well Known Brewery,

I have a brilliant idea for advertising your excellent product and wanted to share it in the hope it might benefit sales.

Yours is an excellent product and one I have been consuming in some quantity since my wife left!

I love the taste. I love the effect.

I have set up my own company and would love the opportunity to make a film to re-launch your beverage

My idea is this:

A new advertising campaign called '**We're Lads**' featuring four twenty something males – Jonny, PJ, Lordy and Squirrel. The four are never seen without a can or pint of your product as we watch them get off with girls in sweaty clubs and fight with aggressive, small minded locals.

Scene One of the ad features the lads in Jonny's lounge. The music is loud, cans of beer litter the coffee table. A banterous comment is aimed at Squirrel's famously small genitals. Everyone laughs. PJ calls for hush, necks his beer and shouts 'COME ON. WE'RE LADS!'

Scene Two – Lordy's eyes swim in and out of focus as he wakes up in a strange bedroom and immediatley fills a sink with vomit. Lordy calls Squirrel from a girl's bed and boasts about his antics. Squirrel puts Lordy on speakerphone and Lordy tells them what happened.

The advert ends with the caption – **We're lads** or **we're f****g lads** if you can get it past the watchdog!

In terms of longevity the idea is durable – the story could be continually evolving. Follow up ads might focus on changes to the lad's personal lives, for example:

A night out is planned but Lordy breaks his leg in a drunken jape and doesn't turn up. The other three lads sit in the pub trying their best but it just isn't the same without Lordy.

Two years later Squirrel and PJ have regular girlfriends and refuse to come out at all. Lordy and Jonny sit in a pub drinking, desperately trying to convince themselves they're still lads.

Ten years later all four lads are married and have lost touch. Totally out of the blue Lordy gets divorced and calls the lads. They hold a reunion jaunt in Krakow, where Lordy goes completely off the rails and sleeps with a beautiful prostitute, who happens to be the girlfriend of a local gangster. In a taxi speeding to the airport with the gangster in pursuit, Lordy suddenly shouts 'We're lads!' and the others break down crying.

I do hope my ideas are of interest to you and I look forward to your response

Kind Regards

Roy Greavesly

Mr Roy Greavesly,
Velvet Sky Film,

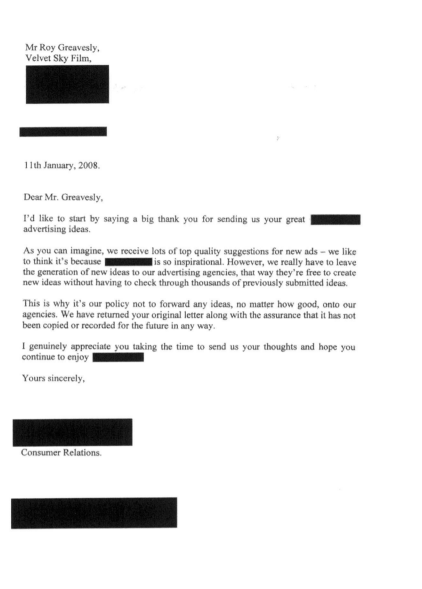

11th January, 2008.

Dear Mr. Greavesly,

I'd like to start by saying a big thank you for sending us your great ▮▮▮▮ advertising ideas.

As you can imagine, we receive lots of top quality suggestions for new ads – we like to think it's because ▮▮▮▮ is so inspirational. However, we really have to leave the generation of new ideas to our advertising agencies, that way they're free to create new ideas without having to check through thousands of previously submitted ideas.

This is why it's our policy not to forward any ideas, no matter how good, onto our agencies. We have returned your original letter along with the assurance that it has not been copied or recorded for the future in any way.

I genuinely appreciate you taking the time to send us your thoughts and hope you continue to enjoy ▮▮▮▮

Yours sincerely,

Consumer Relations.

To A Manufacturer Of Quality Cars

Monday 12th November 2007

Dear Sir or Madam

I am writing on behalf of my wife with a sincere request regarding the specifications of my new car.

My wife has long dreamed of mine owning one of your cars and I am now in a position financially to purchase one for my upcoming birthday. I have yet to settle on the exact model I would like to buy but am clear about the specifications I wish the car to have.

My wife has rather poor eyesight, which she has long attempted to correct with the aid of her optician. She recently ended her ten year association with contact lenses, which she considers overly fiddly and she is loath to wear glasses again. Therefore would it be possible to have my new car fitted with windows adapted to her exact eye prescription?

This is of vital importance with regard to the passenger side as the areas in which my wife typically instructs me to park the car are usually dimly lit (our local rugby club after dark being one example) and my wife will require clear vision through the window at all times.

I fully expect there to be an additional cost implication but know this specification to be entirely necessary in respect of my wife's happiness.

I thank you for taking time to acknowledge this sincere request.

I am, yours most sincerely

Roy Greavesly

23rd November 2007.

Dear Mr Greavesly

Thank you for your recent letter to ██████ with your request for a bespoke specification on a ████████████████ division has an unrivalled expertise in the provision of bespoke requirements for our customers and our team of craftspeople create unique cars every day for our most demanding owners around the world.

The key issues that we have to take into consideration are the feasibility, legality and safety of features that we fit onto our cars. Your request is an insurmountable challenge on all three counts I am afraid. While an interesting concept, it is simply not possible to achieve.

You are presenting a challenge that neither we nor any other vehicle manufacturer is able to meet. If we can assist with the detailed specification of a ██████ with regular glass then my team and I would be happy to assist.

Yours sincerely,

'THUNDERCLAP' – A DIVORCE DIARY

I shuffled out to the recycling bin awash with depression. After disposing of my empty alcohol containers I noticed the man next door washing his car. Having yet to meet my new neighbours, I attempted a smile but despair overwhelmed me. The man's returning smile faded as he noticed my distress. Then he did the strangest thing – he pulled down his trousers and began pretending to have sex with his car.

I laughed hysterically as he humped away, pausing for a nano second to shout 'I LOVE MY CAR!' and flash me a beaming smile before resuming with vigour. I laughed even harder when a woman came from his house and reprimanded him. He threw his bucket of water over her in response. Her face took on a thunderous hue and she marched back inside, returning moments later with her own bucket of water, which she threw over the man. He had used the time to refill and was ready with a second bucket which drenched her and again she retreated.

Seeing me laughing, he trained his garden hose on me. I got a soaking and ran inside to fill my own bucket with which I doused him moments after the woman had again done the same. He sprayed his hose upon us both in retaliation until all three of us were stood on the driveway laughing, soaking wet.

"Hello, my name is Rikkesh and this is my wife Pasmita, would you like to come to my bi-monthly barbecue?" he said.

I smiled and shook their hands. What began as a dark day had considerably brightened. From that day forward whenever Rikkesh saw me on the driveway, his eyes would come alive with mischief. And he would start humping his car.

To A Well Known Train Company

Thursday 3rd January 2008

Dear Train Company Customer Service,

I am writing to offer my unique assistance to your on-board customer service team with regard to resolving face to face disputes with difficult customers.

In my previous role as Customer Service Manager at a well known bank I had the occasion to address angry, aggressive and abusive customers face to face five days a week, fifty weeks of the year. I know what works and I would welcome the opportunity to demonstrate my techniques on board your service.

I have no doubt you will see their effectiveness immediately – perhaps they could then be rolled out as a foundation stone of staff training?

Let me explain my 'General Zod technique.'

There is a difficult customer on board who is travelling without a ticket. He wants to buy a ticket onboard but has been roused to anger after being informed there are no discounted fares available and that he will be required to pay the full single amount. The argument is getting heated.

I stride over to the difficult customer dressed as General Zod from the film 'Superman 2.' Leather jump suit, small goatee beard, chest hair exposed below pale, almost translucent skin and knee length leather boots. With authority radiating from my beard, I look him firmly in the eye and say 'Take my hand. Kneel before Zod.'

He kneels. I explain that he will have to pay the full fare. He hands over the cash and returns to his seat, a little bit dazed but otherwise unharmed.

I would be happy to demonstrate this technique as part of your staff training and improve your excellent rail service further.

I feel that not to do so would be a missed opportunity and would almost certainly incur my wrath.

Yours most sincerely

Roy Greavesly [AKA 'General Zod']

17 January 2008

Mr R Greavesly

Dear Mr Greavesly,

Thank you very much for your correspondence, which we received in this office on 11 January 2008.

I was most grateful to receive your comments and suggestions regarding the training provided for our our-board staff.

Your feedback is important to us, and we hope to welcome you on board again soon.

Yours sincerely

Customer Relations Team Leader

Monday 21st January 2008

Dear Rachel,

Thankyou for your letter [REF – 4756791.] The General was most disappointed to hear that you appear to have rejected his offer to train all of your staff in his 'General Zod technique.'

I am sorry to inform you that you have incurred The General's wrath. When The General read your letter he was so incensed he went into the garden, fell to his knees and screamed to the heavens. Until the rain came.

When The General came back inside he was pensive and soaked to the bone. He paced back and forth in the kitchen, both forefingers pressed to his lips. After precisely one hour, he stopped.

The General ordered me to reply to your letter and to stress that he is not normally a forgiving man, but on this occasion this reaction is most expedient vis a vis 'Operation Wrath.'

I must inform you that The General will soon be in control of Planet Earth and will be seeking a small staff of those committed to his rule. The General admires your backbone and would like to offer you a position on his staff.

Would you wish you to accept this?

The General foresees your reluctance to relinquish your current salary and status but anticipates that his offer of making you ruler of the country of your choice will be tempting enough.

I must advise you to reply promptly, The General is not renowned for his patience. Wrath, yes. Patience? No.

Yours most sincerely

Olga The Impassive, First Secretary to General Zod.

To A Tourist Board

Tuesday 8th January 2008

Good Morning,

I am writing on behalf of the band I manage – Velvet Sky – to ask if we might be able to shoot the video for the band's first single with your iconic castle as a backdrop.

Velvet Sky are a Nottingham band comprised of four lads who have recently signed to Emotive Records with myself as their manager.

We are seeking a venue to shoot the video of *Talk For England* and hope our proposal is agreeable. The song is about the necessary death of celebrity culture and its video will feature the band and a pointless celebrity who will have little idea what's going on.

The pointless celebrity will be stood on a podium talking to a group of journalists about how talented they are. Notes are taken, flashbulbs go off and excitement grows. Then an arrow hits the celebrity in the chest and kills them.

The camera pulls back to reveal Lordy, Velvet Sky's lead singer dressed as Robin Hood holding his bowstring taut.The screen fades to black.

We will of course contact other locations if necessary, but wanted to contact you in the first instance as the band are complete LAD's and your castle would be their number one choice.

Yours most sincerely

Roy Greavesly

Friday 11th January 2008

Roy Greavesly
Velvet Sky
███████████████

Dear Roy

Thank you for your letter regarding the possibility of filming your band's video in our grounds. This is certainly a possibility, but we would need to know more details about what it involves, when you would like to film and how long it is likely to take. For any filming in the grounds we charge an admin fee of £75.00.

If you could let us have a phone number or e-mail address for you it would make negotiations easier. I am only in the office Thursdays and Fridays, but if you need to speak to someone on any other day, please contact ████████ ████████████

I look forward to hearing from you.

Kind regards

Monday 21st January 2008

RE: Request for filming information.

Good Morning,

Thank you so much for your positive response regarding the filming of '**Talk For England**' – the forthcoming single from Velvet Sky.

I now enclose further details on our filming requirements.

Firstly, I am pleased to announce that the video will be directed by Peter Yehuda. Peter is a Bafta winner and veteran of short film, having first cut his teeth on Eastenders.

With Peter in charge we anticipate the shoot will wrap within two hours. We would like to film this Tuesday February 12th.

We are open to suggestions on a suitable location in the grounds, so long as the castle itself is in view. We have booked a pointless celebrity who has been told that we have organised them a comfortable trailer, constant press attention and six bodyguards. But don't worry - this is a lie! The song is about tearing down celebrity culture after all!

The shoot will involve a small crew of four, plus the lads and Celebrity (9 total) and should cause minimum of fuss. The only fuss we cannot avoid will come at the wrap when Peter Yehuda will insist on running through the grounds shouting 'YEHUDA! YEHUDA! YEHUDA!

On this occasion he has promised not to do this naked. I hope this will cause no offence, Yehuda is committed to his art and this single burst of ego is traditional upon finishing a film.

It is also a mating call.

I do hope this is enough information and that the shoot can now proceed. If you have any objections please reply promptly.

Yours most sincerely

Roy Greavesly

Roy Greavesly
Velvet Sky

Friday 25th January 2008

Dear Roy,

Thank you for your letter. For us to proceed with this any further we need to meet you and discuss your exact requirements. We would be able to arrange this much more efficiently if you could provide us with a contact telephone number rather than corresponding by letter.

As stated in my previous letter there will be a £75.00 admin charge, but depending on the level of assistance you require there may also be additional staffing costs, these things can be discussed when we meet. We will also require you to provide us with a professional running order of the events and timings of the day along with proof of your public liability insurance.

I am not in the office for the next 2 weeks, please contact ▮▮▮▮ the ▮▮▮ Manager on ▮▮▮▮▮▮▮▮▮▮▮▮

Kind regards

VELVET SKY

Monday 11th February 2008

Dear Barry,

I have been in touch with your colleague Lisa and am pleased to now be in correspondence with you. As Lisa has hopefully informed you, I represent local band **Velvet Sky** and we are interested in filming the video for our first single **'Talk For England'** in the castle grounds.

I am happy to supply you with a detailed running order and evidence of public liability insurance, however I am unable to correspond via the telephone due to a phobia I have had for some years.

I am unable to cope with hearing the word 'phalanges,' as hearing it triggers panic attacks I have suffered since the age of fourteen when the word was used by Lee Huyton as a prelude to a violent assault.

The shock of a thicko like Lee Huyton identifying the body part he aimed to damage with the correct medical term made his subsequent assault something of a double whammy.

I may be able to speak to you on the phone, provided you are able to assure me that the word 'phalanges' will not be used during our conversation?

Yours most sincerely

Roy Greavesly

To A Train Company

VELVET SKY

Friday 1st February 2008

Dear Sir or Madam,

I am writing on behalf of the band I manage – Velvet Sky – to ask if you might be keen to assist with the front cover art for the band's first album, due for release in August of this year.

The album is to be called *Neural Pathways* and deals with such themes as the necessary death of celebrity culture. We would like to shoot the album cover at Nottingham Railway station as it is a place of some significance for the lads.

For the shoot we would require the use of a ten metre section of platform that is closed off to the public.

The shot itself will feature the band and their friend Ken, who is a professional lookalike [and huge fan!] of the actor Tom Oliver who plays the character 'Lou Carpenter' in 'Neighbours.'

The photo will feature the band standing around 'Lou' while he lies on a table and gets his buttocks waxed.

We would need one hour max for the shoot and anticipate no disruption whatsoever to rail services. I look forward to your response and hope the proposal is is agreeable.

Yours most sincerely

Roy Greavesly
(Band Manager)

Roy Greavesly

Wed 06 February 2008

Dear Mr Greavesly

Thankyou for your letter regarding Lou Carpenter's buttock-waxing. Sadly we are not in a position to allow this enervating depilatory experience as Nottingham station is run by ▇▇▇▇▇ Trains, not us. You would have to contact them for permission.

Yours sincerely

VELVET SKY

Monday 11th February 2008

Dear Andrew,

Thankyou for your letter dated February 6th regarding shooting of the band's album cover. The Train Company you mentioned have unfortunately put the kibbosh on us shooting on their patch. This is a shame. The lads are keen and Ken [Tom] talks of nothing else. We now need someone with a sense of humour (and a fully operational railway station) to play ball.

Do you feel able to accomodate us at any of the stations under your control? I did say to the lads that such an album cover runs the risk of not being taken at all seriously, but that is the lad's sense of humour and Lou Carpenter is a hero of modern times I'm sure you'll agree?

Andrew, I place the fate of our project in your capable hands.

Yours most sincerely

Roy Greavesly
[Band Manager]

Roy Greavesly

Wed 13 February 2008

Dear Mr Greavesly

Thanks for your letter of 11th February. I'm afraid I can't really bring you any good news.

Sadly I'm told we will have to turn you down as well. If it's any consolation, ▮▮▮▮▮▮▮ doesn't manage any stations east of Tamworth, and we would have had to use the services of a location management company (to keep Tom's bare buttocks away from passengers and trains) which would have cost you £750 an hour.

I'm sorry I can't be more positive. Have you considered Photoshop?

Yours sincerely

VELVET SKY

Monday 7th July 2008

Dear Andrew,

Thankyou for your letter of 13th February regarding the shooting of the band's album cover, which you described as 'an enervating depilatory experience.'

I am sorry for the delay in responding. I have been holed up in the studio with the lads, re-recording 'Neural Pathways.' Due to studio errors (some prat forgot to put the tape in), the album release has been put back and will now hit the shops in November.

We have successfully completed the album artwork featuring Ken as 'Lou Carpenter.' I now write asking for your assistance with the shooting of the album's first single – **Lou Carpenter Goes Crazy On The Dancefloor.**

Would it be possible to shoot the video onboard one of your trains? A script has yet to be finalised, but the basic storyline would see Ken leave his airline seat to dance energetically to the band's single in the aisle (Ken has specifically asked to do this naked!)

As a thankyou for your co-operation, we would like to give your staff (and perhaps yourself?) the opportunity to dance alongside him.

Please advise if this proposal is agreeable and we can discuss the logistics of the shoot.

Yours Sincerely

Roy Greavesly
(Band Manager)

Roy Greavesly

30 July 2008

Dear Mr Greavesly

Thanks for your letter of 8 July and apologies for the delay in replying. Sadly, naked Tom Oliver is not for us.

We don't allow video shooting on any of our trains, regardless of creed, colour, or clothing. Dancing is frowned upon. Nudity is more than frowned upon. So the combination of a videoing a naked dancing man is really a non starter.

I'm sorry I can't be more positive. Have you considered CGI?

Yours sincerely

VELVET SKY

Monday 4th August 2008

Dear Andrew,

I thankyou sincerely for your letter dated 30th July and am sorry that once again you have had to disappoint us.

There are no hard feelings however and I would like to invite you to an enormous party on September 6th to send the lad's off on their nationwide tour.

We have hired <u>Hell On Earth</u> Bar and Grill here in Nottingham and will transform it Velvet Sky style. There will beer, chicken wings and burgers, *Neighbours* episodes played on a loop on the giant screen and Lou Carpenter themed drinking games (basically everytime Lou appears onscreen you have to down a shot!)

I would like to invite you and any colleagues to this event (perhaps you could charter a bus and pull into the carpark en masse?) The party will continue at <u>Rhubarb</u> where the lad's will be *feted*, to use a lovely word.

We will also have one of those inflatable boxing rings in the <u>Hell On Earth</u> car park.

Perhaps you and I could trade jabs with massive gloves? Or perhaps you could nominate a champion and I could nominate a champion and the loser would have to dye his hair grey like Lou!

Please RSVP with estimated numbers and I will add you guys to the guestlist.

Yours Sincerely

Roy Greavesly
[Band Manager]

To An Important Man

VELVET SKY

Tuesday 8th January 2008

Dear Important Man,

I am writing on behalf of the band I manage – Velvet Sky – to ask if you might be keen to feature in the front cover art for the band's first single, due for release in August of this year.

'Velvet Sky' are a Nottingham band comprised of four local boys who have recently signed to Emotive Records with myself as their manager.

The single is to be called *Neural Pathways* and deals with such themes as the necessary death of celebrity culture. We have gained permission to shoot the cover art for the first single at the local Leisure Centre in March.

For the shoot the swimming pool will be drained of water and pumped full of custard. Lordy, the lead singer, will be submerged in the custard with a chokehold on a pointless celebrity.

Also in shot will be a set of cricket stumps, a Notts Forest crest (the lads are big fans) and a small likeness of Robin Hood.

We very much wanted to ask if you, as an important man, would be prepared to stand poolside and be part of the shot?

I do appreciate the demands on your time must be many but myself and the lads would consider it an honour to have you on the cover when the record hits the shops.

Yours most sincerely

Roy Greavesly

HOUSE OF COMMONS
LONDON SW1A 0AA

11th February, 2008

Dear Mr. Greavesly,

████████████ has asked me to write and thank you for your letter of 8th January, inviting him to be featured in the front cover art for Velvet Sky's first single. I am sorry you have not had an earlier response.

████████████ did consider your request. It is certainly an unusual one and it is the first time he has been asked to feature on the cover of a single in this way. However, on reflection, I am afraid he has decided that it really will not be possible for him to agree to this. As you appreciate, there are many demands on his time and it is simply not possible for him to fit all the requests he receives into his diary, however intriguing they might be.

He has asked me to send his apologies to the band and wish them every success on the release of their single later this year.

Yours sincerely,

████████████

PA to Rt. Hon. ████████████

Mr. Roy Greavesley,
Velvet Sky,
████████████

'THUNDERCLAP' – A DIVORCE DIARY

Gary turned up at my house tonight. He told me I'd better stop calling Karen because he knows some really hard gangsters. He didn't take kindly to my observation that professional gangsters probably have better things to do than become embroiled in marital disputes. My riposte confused him. All he could think to do was punch me in the face. Round one to me.

Gary sent a DVD round today. It showed him and Karen having sexual intercourse. Gary had added a rather bombastic commentary to the extras. He might've thought Karen was enjoying herself, but I was with her for eleven years. Her acting may have fooled Gary, but it failed to convince me. Round two to Greavesly!

For seventeen consecutive mornings I poo on Gary's doorstep. I am eventually caught when Gary contracts a techno boffin to install CCTV. I get an official police warning for harrassment. He has to clean the poo off the step. Round three to Roy! Someone stop the bout before the lad gets hurt!

Gary called round again today. He looked angry so I decided to pre-empt any threatening behavior.

Before he could address me I ran onto the front lawn, flapping my arms and shouted "I'M THE PIGEON! I'M THE PIGEON!"

"You're an' 'eadcase man. You're an' 'eadcase!" he spluttered. Then Gary got back in his car and drove away.

I never saw him again.

'The Custard Directive' – A Psychological Thriller
By Roy Greavesly

The man at the controls of the helicopter thought they were mad. "This plan is nuts man. Like, hey man, you're crazy." The answering voice cracked like a whip and the pilot quieted. One of the passengers gave a thumbs up to the other. All was again well. The helicopter flew south west from Nottingham, landed briefly on an industrial estate in Tamworth to attach its cargo, then flew above the M6 heading for Wolverhampton. The stakes were high. There was tension in the air.

When the plot had been conceived three days before at a bi-monthly barbecue, it had been laughed off as a jokey sideswipe from a recently divorced man who had found abundant solace in alcohol. But now they were airborne and the drunken man was very sober indeed.

Roy Greavesly stared with a frightening intensity towards the rows of houses ahead. Having memorised the pictures on Google Earth he knew exactly which house to aim for and he directed the pilot there. As the house came into view the tension reached fever pitch. Nothing could go wrong. There was no room for error!

Greavesly directed the pilot to hold steady just above the house. The pilot obeyed, holding the joystick firm, wanting nothing more than to get the mission over with and never see these two lunatics again. On Greavesly's pre-arranged signal – a loud raspberry, the pilot flipped the switch. The large vat they were carrying opened at its base and several gallons of custard hit the roof of the house with a splash and began oozing down.

"GO GO GO!" Roy Greavesly bellowed and the helicopter veered sharply away. Greavesly laughed hysterically as he ripped down his trousers and began to squash his bum cheeks against the window – a further act of defiance.

"NO ROY. NO!" his next door neighbour Rikkesh cried, fighting to restrain him. "You've done enough Roy. You've done enough!" "YES" thought Roy Greavesly as he looked back at his ex-wife's new house, now dripping with custard, a yellow blot in the distance, "I've done enough."

To a TV Company

Tuesday 1st July 2008

Dear Martin,

I am writing to suggest the release of a brilliant new Sports DVD called '**TV Cameramen Select.**'

Whenever I have watched sport on TV I have noticed the uncanny ability of cameramen to identify attractive women in the crowd and focus their lens on them for uncomfortable lengths of time [do they attend a special training school to learn this by the way?] My DVD idea is for a compilation package of the most attractive women ever captured in the crowd by TV Cameramen at UK sporting events.

Perhaps the top one hundred women from the Test Match, Wimbledon, Match of the Day, the Grand National and other events could be included?

I have a personal collection of 55 video tapes and have compiled a shortlist of 178 women, dating back to The 1989 Open Golf championship and I would be more than happy to sit on the judging panel and help put this together. I would also suggest myself as presenter.

I do hope that you appreciate this suggestion as I feel it would be a hugely popular release and I look forward very much to your thoughts on my proposal.

Yours Sincerely

Roy Greavesly

Mr Greavesly

28th July 2008

Dear Mr Greavesly

Thank you for suggesting 'Cameraman Select.' I am sorry to say I do not share your enthusiasm for the commercial viability of your project.

Kind regards

To a Producer of Tea

Wednesday 9th July 2008

Dear Sir or Madam,

A recent discovery has led to increased enjoyment of my tea.

I was walking down the stairs with a cuppa in hand (your brand of course) and being impatiently thirsty I took a sip. My nose entered the tea. This was surprisingly pleasant.

I now use nothing but my nose to stir my tea. Other friends have followed suit and it's become something of a craze in our middle class enclave. Have I stumbled across a phenomenon? Do you know of any other people who routinely use their noses to stir their tea?

I began using an anti-clockwise motion, but have found through experimentation that clockwise is best.

I am in the process of setting up a website for nose stirring enthusiasts and wanted to ask if a prominent member of your brand (one of the big bods basically) would contribute a quote to the homepage, or possibly even send in a photo of themselves using their nose to stir their tea?

When the site is completed it will have a live webcam to my desk where people from around the globe, on the hour, every hour, can watch me stir my tea with my nose!

I am tremendously excited by this idea and would love to hear your thoughts.

Yours most sincerely

Roy Greavesly

PS: My wife Karen would have hated me stirring my tea with my nose, but since she left me it's no longer a problem!

Mr R Greavesly

Dear Mr Greavesly

Thank you for your letter.

I was very interested in your discovery which I must admit is quite unusual. It is surprising how the greatest discoveries can evolve from accidental incidents.

However, as your theory is based on ████ tea, I wondered if the results would be the same for ████. (The company you actually wrote to) Maybe there would be a difference in your findings. To this end, and purely in the matter of balanced research, I am sending you a pack of ' ████ tea bags to trial.

I would be interested to hear more of your research and look forward to seeing your website. Can't wait to see this magnificent proboscis!

Yours sincerely

Consumer Services Advisor

Tuesday 5th August 2008

Dear Sally,

I just emerged from my laboratory after rigorous testing of the Tea Bags you kindly donated (I have not slept for three days!)

I'm sure you will be delighted to hear that your brand stands up well. They outperformed Brand A by 18% in the ease of stirring test and Brand C by 22% in the swimsuit round. I regret to say they were disappointing in the squat thrusts – losing out to Brand B by 88 thrusts to 49. I had to subtract marks from Brand B for racism and homophobia however.

In more general testing your brand was a tremendously enjoyable dip. I held my nose in for an average of 32 seconds on each cup and on 79 cups, returned to dip a second and third time (1 cup got a fly in it, which put me off!) I also found your brand to have a powerful clearing effect on my sinuses – perhaps you could branch into the Flu Remedy racket and challenge the market leaders for majority market share?

I found the steam from the bags also pleasant, with a lovely exfoliating effect. Your brand was unusual as its taste was improved by a clockwise stir, every other brand was the opposite. So your tea bags are not afraid to be individual, which was most interesting to me.

Thank you very much for your encouragement and for your enquiry into the website. It is currently under construction (lab testing is time consuming as I'm sure you appreciate). The moment the site is launched I will let you know.

I would enjoy hearing your thoughts on the test results and have one further question; if I were to construct a pair of underpants made entirely of tea bags, could I have my photo taken for your website and/or newsletter?

Yours Sincerely

Roy Greavesly

PS: I say 'if.' In fact, I am wearing them this very moment!

'THUNDERCLAP' – A DIVORCE DIARY

Today was a momentous day. Today I realised that Karen isn't coming back. Today I realised that this is a good thing. Today I realised I am free. Today I stood on the garden wall at my next door neighbour's bi-monthly barbecue and belted out the song 'Looking For Freedom' – a cover of the David Hasselhoff classic. I got halfway through the second verse before Rikkesh could coax me down.

Today, with Rikkesh's encouragement, I signed up to a dating website. My profile picture – an action shot of Karen's new house dripping with custard has proved an exciting talking point and I have been approached by a woman with the username 'MadCow37.'

A second woman, Imogen, looks more promising. Her profile picture – a photoshopped effort of her and the actor Alan Rickman certainly caught my eye. Although what she was doing to 'Alan Rickman' in subsequent photoshopped pictures wouldn't be at all welcome in a family newspaper. Anyhow, we're going a date.

To A Reputable Hotel

Monday 15th December 2008

Dear Sir or Madam,

I am hoping to book a weekend at your hotel. Prior to making a booking I wonder if you might reassure me over a potentially upsetting matter.

I am concerned that, should I make a booking, the actor Alan Rickman will arrive the same afternoon also seeking a room.

Since the infamous divorce from Karen, I have met a new partner called Imogen and have no wish to lose her to the overwhelming charm of such a famous artiste.

I know I could never measure up. Five minutes in the bar telling *Die Hard* anecdotes and Imogen would be pawing at Rickman's trousers.

To further illustrate my concern, I include some further information about Imogen:

- Imogen has a Professor Snape tattoo on the small of her back.
- Imogen starts each day with a 6am salutation to Rickman (involving candles, chanting and everything.)
- Everytime we watch the end of *Die Hard*, Imogen hurls herself at the TV as Rickman plummets from the window in slow motion in the hope of saving him. This is despite her having seen the film 852 times.

I am concerned that Rickman might arrive last minute, paying heed to an actorly whim. Could I please have your assurance that should Rickman turn up, he will be denied access to the hotel?

It is very important that I enjoy time alone with Imogen and I am determined to deny Rickman the chance to make a late play for her affections. It would be devastating to witness him wooing her over a silver tongued *Claret Les Deux Brasseurs.*

I do hope that you understand my anxiety and are able to help.

Yours most sincerely

Roy Greavesly

Mr Roy Greavesly ███████████████████████

███████████████

Bracknell, 18.12.2008

Dear Mr Greavesly

Thank you very much for your letter dated 15th December 2008.

Mr Rickman has not stayed with as in the past and does not have a booking in the future. Further it is well known that during the winter month he usually resides in Hogwarts.

In addition to that we would like to inform you that our Reception Manager is far more superior in looks and smartness. This might however cause an upsetting matter. Also we have to inform you that candles, for whatever celebration, and loud chanting are not allowed in bedrooms. The Pay TV program does not offer any movies with Mr Rickman at this stage.

We also do not deny access to any customer with or without a wand in their possession. On the other hand Bruce Willis pops in from time to time, which I hope does not affect you decision.

Nevertheless, we have included a brochure and one of our reservation agents will be more than happy to help with any booking.

Mr Greavesly, we are looking very much forward to welcome you in the near future and we would like to wish you and Imogen a Merry R-free Christmas and a Happy New Year.

With Kind Regards

██████████████████

Rooms Division Manager

To Several Lord Mayor's

Monday 5th January 2009

Dear Lord Mayor,

Does the idea of proving your superiority over other Lord Mayor's excite? I am writing to invite you to participate in a very prestigious event – the inaugral 'Iron-Mayor' contest, which will be held on the weekend of April 11th/12th 2009 in Blackpool (Venue TBC).

Every Lord Mayor in the United Kingdom has been extended the opportunity to prove themselves the number one. We very much hope you will add your name to an ever growing list of entrants.

Each Mayor will be required to contest a challenging series of events – all designed to assess a wide range of skills. Points will be awarded throughout. The victor, and 'Iron-Mayor' champion will be the Mayor with the highest points total.

Please refer overleaf for a list of events. Travel expenses and accomodation will be covered for each Mayor and their partner of choice.

We anticipate a strong field and would encourage you to confirm or decline your participation as soon as possible.

We look forward to welcoming you.

Kind Regards

Roy Greavesly
(Event Organiser)

'IRON-MAYOR 2009' – LIST OF EVENTS

- **DRESSAGE:** A catwalk stroll in full regalia.

- **CIGARS BY THE POOL:** Mayor's don swimshorts and make polite conversation with assorted poolside guests. Points scaled according to wittiness of banter.

- **36 HOLE STABLEFORD:** Points awarded for outstanding golf and garishness of dress.

- **HECKLE PUT DOWN:** Mayor's perform the speech of their choice as various heckles are voiced by audience members. Unlike comedy clubs, ALL heckles will be of a gentle nature, for example, 'Why do we have to pay council tax? I don't want to pay it!' OR 'when are you going to sort out parking in the town centre?' Top marks will be awarded to the best heckle putdown.

- **SPEED DATING:** Mayor with the most ticks after thirty minutes is the winner. [Spousal disclaimer: Mayor's will not be expected to go on real dates. All of the women participants will be actors.]

• **IMPROMPTU HOEDOWN:** Mayor's perform an impromptu hoedown on the topic of our choice. To allow some advance preparation, topics will be chosen from the list below:

Why are so many people self-serving, spoonfed, desensitised idiots who live life blind, have no ambition and do nothing to improve the world we live in?

• **RANT YOURSELF RED:** A two minute rant on each Mayor's issue of choice. Full marks awarded for a well argued grievance culminating in a rising crescendo of rage.

• **NODDY HOLDER CHAMBER:** Mayor's will be placed in a sealed chamber with Noddy Holder. How much Noddy Holder can you stand? Top marks for the Mayor who lasts longest.

Mr Roy Greavesly
Event Organiser

███████████████

8 January 2009

Dear Mr Greavesly

The Mayor, Cllr ███████████ has asked me to thank you for your kind invitation to the "Iron-Mayor" Contest taking place in Blackpool in April. Unfortunately, he is unable to attend this event due to other engagements, but hopes it is a great success.

With kind regards.

Yours sincerely

███████████████

Assistant to the Mayor

'THUNDERCLAP' – A DIVORCE DIARY

I write this in the hope of alleviating my confusion over a music video I watched today. The video in question is **Jump In My Car** by David Hasselhoff and I desperately need to understand what it's about.

The video features 'The Hoff' driving his car along a back alley at two o'clock in the morning in pursuit of a pretty girl.

The Hoff offers her a lift *because it's too far to walk home on her own* and the girl politely but firmly says NO several times. The Hoff continues to pressure her and alludes to his *Knight Rider* fame in a bid to persuade her. Eventually the girl agrees to accept a lift if he promises to keep his hands to himself.

But once The Hoff learns that the girl lives eighty-four miles away he orders her out of his car and then, in a complete role reversal, she starts pressuring *him*, suggesting that if he does give her a lift they could go out on a date next week.

The Hoff refuses and the girl says that she thought he said he was a nice guy and the Hoff abruptly tells her that he isn't and drives off. Essentially that is what happens. But what does it all mean? I have some questions:

1. Why does the Hoff only allude to his role in Knightrider and ignore his success in single handedly bringing down Communism by singing *Looking For Freedom* atop the Berlin Wall?
2. How does the girl correctly estimate the distance from the alleyway to her home as eighty-four miles? And why does she ignore all known common sense about personal safety by walking alone down a dark alleyway at two o'clock in the morning?
3. What's going on?

To a Casting Agency

Friday 9th January 2009

Dear Sir or Madam,

My ex-wife Karen is visiting soon for a clear the air tete a tete and I plan to stage a play in my front room to surprise her.

I have re-decorated my living room into an exact replica of the wartime cafe in the classic BBC Comedy 'Allo, Allo' [complete with bootleg painting of 'The Fallen Madonna With Ze Big Boobies.]

I now require a suitable cast of 'Allo, Allo' characters to bring my play to life. I myself will portray Rene Artois and must insist upon a very attractive brunette to growl at me in a primal manner whenever Karen isn't looking.

I would also like a 'Monsieur Alfonse' [Oh, my dicky ticker!], an 'Officer Crabtree' [Good Moaning] and a 'Herr Flick' of the Gestapo. I will not require a 'General von Klinkerhoffen' as the man across the street is a spit image and I have agreed to take a shower with him in exchange for him dusting off his uniform.

I will however need a 'Madame Edith' as the plan is as follows:

When Karen enters, 'Rene' will give everyone pieces of cheese with which to stop up their ears as 'Edith' begins to sing. Karen however, will not get any cheese!!!

With your help I can show her that I have truly moved on. It will also be extremely funny – Karen *hates* 'Allo, Allo!' Whenever it came on she used to throw things at the telly!

I have even written a little script for the characters and am happy to send this if it will help persuade your artistes to accept the job!

I very much hope you can help facilitate this. Time is of the essence and I would appreciate a speedy quotation.

Yours Sincerely

Roy Greavesly

Roy Greavsley

13th January 2008

Dear Roy

Thank you for your letter.

Unfortunately we are not able to assist with this, as ▮▮▮▮ do only deal with professional projects for our professional actors.

Apologies for any disappointment and I do wish you great success with this.

Kind regards

To A Funeral Organiser

Friday 9th January 2009

Dear Sir or Madam,

Recent media coverage of Harold Pinter's funeral service has turned my thoughts towards the depressing inevitability of my own death.

I would therefore like to book the arrangements for my funeral in advance. Hopefully <u>well</u> in advance, but you never can tell!

Pinter's funeral was rather theatrical in bent. He had The Great Gambon perform readings from his plays in church. Following this, Pinter's wife approached the newly berthed casket and spoke the words 'Farewell thy sweet prince,' affording the service a dramaticly appropriate and dignified full stop.

Whilst I cannot count on The Great Gambon to lament my demise, I have been inspired by The Great Pinter and wish to arrange a funeral with the following component parts, a wish list of sorts

My wishlist is as follows:

• Brian Blessed to appear in character as Portugese football supremo 'Gugarin,' who destroys the England team's boastful ego's by making them all work as taxi drivers in Grimsby for six months.

• Hymms to be replaced with a fervent rendition of Slade's 'Lock Up Your Daughters.'

• The Aidan Dunbar Male Voice Choir to recite the lyrics to Queen: 'Bohemian Rhapsody' in a Birmingham accent.

• I would like to be dressed by the undertaker thus:

1.   Comfortable 'Lou Carpenter' slacks.
2.   Iron grey (dyed if I have died before it has gone grey) 'Lou Carpenter' hair with side parting.
3.   Denim 'Lou Carpenter' shirt with three quarter length sleeves, rolled fashionably to represent fortitide, charm and business sense in the strong forearms and wrists.

That is all.

Would it be possible to firmly book these arrangements? I am happy to pay in advance with perhaps an inflation adjusted dividend paid from my estate in the year of the actual service?

I hope you will not see my request as too unusual. It is necessary to do this. If the service is left to my sister in Grantham it will be a <u>completely drab affair</u>.

Yours Sincerely

Roy Greavesly

26 Jan. 09

Dear Mr Greavesly,

Thank you for your letter, forwarded to me from  seeking to pre-plan your own funeral.

The concept of pre-planning and/or pre-paying one's funeral in advance is not a new one. One of the benefits is that it affords the planner an opportunity to tailor make their funeral in a way that best reflects their needs, means and personality and allows the surviving family the satisfaction that the "final ceremony" is just what the deceased wanted.

A particularly interesting aspect to the funeral of Harold Pinter was the uniqueness and specificity to him as an individual and the involvement of friends and associates who had been important, to him, during his life. It was absolutely fitting that the funeral was a "theatrical event" but I do not think that that could be replicated for any other individual.

I have attempted to deal with each of your requests in chronological order:

- Brian Blessed, would be unlikely to honour your wish unless you have a personal connection with him.

- As a funeral does not have to be a religious ceremony you are at liberty to choose whatever music you want.

- Aidan Dunbar male voice choir may be available, at a price.

- Dressing and presentation can be honoured exactly as per your wishes, if your wish is to be cremated then clothing must be of natural material i.e cotton, silk or wool. Shoes would not be cremated.

It is entirely possible to draw up a plan for you taking the aforementioned points into consideration. The funeral directors charges (ours) would be fixed if payment is made in advance and the disbursements would be paid, at today`s rate, as a "contribution" balance payable at time of need.

It will be necessary to meet with you if you wish to proceed with a funeral plan.Please do not hesitate to contact me should you wish to discuss the matter further.

Yours sincerely,

To A Supermarket Chain

Thursday 5th February 2009

Dear Sir or Madam,

No doubt you will have heard about the dramatic events surrounding my visit to your Loughborough store this Monday.

I am writing to apologise for these events.

Basically, my name is Roy Greavesly and I am divorced.

My ex-wife Karen tried to strip my finances bare in a bid for a more extravagant lifestyle with her new partner Gary. He is not very bright. Luckily I hired a solicitor to tackle her demands. I won't bore you with the legal jargon, but in essence we told her to sod off.

As a further gesture of defiance, I attached a weighty sack of custard to a friend's helicopter, hovered above Karen's house and left her new abode dripping in a tasty yellow goo.

Things calmed down after that.

And so we come to Monday's events. In my defence I must state that my outburst was not intended to offend anyone.

Yes, I pulled off my shirt leaving my torso bare.

Yes, I ran through the store, shouting 'ROY, ROY, ROY!'

Yes, I accidentally upset a pyramid of Coco Pops.

But my display was an expression of pure joy.

I have finally accepted that me and Karen are finito.

I am free.

I AM FREE!

And that is the only reason I stripped off.

But I do appreciate that some shoppers were particularly startled. I made an immediate apology to the store manager who was kind enough to allow me to broadcast an apology to fellow shoppers over the PA system.

I would now like to extend an apology to you. Would you be so kind as to cascade my apology through your organisation?

I have written my adventures into a book and hope to get this published. Can I count on you to display some copies in your stores?

Yours Sincerely

Roy Greavesly

Our reference: ███████

16 February 2009

Mr Roy Greavesly
█████████

Dear Mr Greavesly

Thank you for your letter. I appreciate you contacting us to apologise for your outburst in our ██████████ store. I also understand you would like us to stock your book, once it is published.

I am grateful for letting us know the reasons why you felt you had to act that way when you shopped with us. I realise that ████████████ the Store Manager, gave you the opportunity to apologise to the customers straight away. We really appreciate this and will of course be happy to welcome you in our store in the future.

We are credible book and magazine outlet and we aim to meet the demands of our wide range of customers. In some stores, we do sell books by local authors. However, at this stage I am unable to guarantee that we will stock your book. I suggest you contact us when you make specific arrangements with the publishers. We will then be happy to consider offering your book in our store.

Thank you again for taking the time to write. I would like to wish you a lot of success with your writing career.

Yours sincerely

Customer Manager

To A Travel Company

Thursday 5th February 2009

Dear Sir or Madam,

I write in the hope you may aid my pursuit of sun, sand, sea and adventure.

I need to escape this abominable weather and the crunch of both credit and snow.

I would like a two week break abroad where I plan to showcase my collection of thongs. I would like a five star hotel at a lively resort. Nightlife is a priority as I wish to drink heavily.

Yours Sincerely

Roy Greavesly

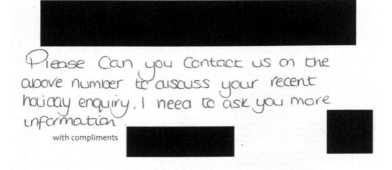

Please Can you Contact us on the above number to discuss your recent holiday enquiry, I need to ask you more information.

with compliments

Monday 23rd February 2009

Dear Amy,

Thankyou for your response to my holiday enquiry. I must congratulate you on your handwriting, it was most pleasing to the eye. I have an impediment that has left me unable to use the phone and wonder if it will be possible to make my holiday arangements through the old fashioned medium of a letter?

Our telephone conversation may begin promisingly, but at some point, and for no apparent reason, I will suddenly go 'Ruuurrrraaarrrrrrgggghhhhhhhh!!!!' This is an unfortunate side effect from a dream I had recently about John Prescott.

In the dream, I was happily asleep in a strange room when the light came on and I saw John Prescott coming towards me. Though his steps were lumbering and deliberate, I was terrified and powerless to move as his big football face loomed over me and he pursed his lips for a kiss.

As Prescott's jowls wobbled mere inches from my face, survival instinct kicked in and I woke up screaming.

The dream continues to revisit me in my waking hours, hence the sudden outbursts.

I dare not drive my car at present and do not want to risk shouting 'Ruuuuurrrraaaarrrrrrgghhhhhh!' over the phone as I would not wish to alarm you in any way. I do however realise that you may need further information to find me a suitable trip.

To pre-empt your questions therefore, I supply the following information:

• I would like a two week holiday in March at a foreign location costing a maximum of £1,000. There should be a nearby beach of suitable length to allow me a good five minute stroll while parading my thongs.

I do hope it will be acceptable to correspond by letter.

Yours sincerely

Roy Greavesly

'THUNDERCLAP' – A DIVORCE DIARY

Six weeks ago [at Rikkesh's urging] I joined a gym. Six weeks later I have compiled a list of complaints based on the bizarre behaviour encountered in the men's changing room. I have decided to name this list **Greavesly's Grievances** and have listed my grievances below.

Grievance Number 1:

Men weighing themselves naked, often bending from the waist to set the scales whilst standing on them, thereby framing between their legs any spherical, dangly objects for the displeasure of anyone with the misfortune to look their way at the wrong moment.

Solution: Remove the scales. Put up a sign requesting that underwear is worn whilst using the scales [let's face it - it makes little difference to the result - these people are not professional athletes or boxers trying to make weight.]

Grievance Number 2:

Men treating the toilets and sink area as if it is their personal bathroom at home. Last week I walked in on a man standing naked at the sink, his face lathered with foam, having a shave in nothing but a pair of flip flops. Why was he naked in the toilets? He's in a public place, not his executive suite at the Radisson Hotel, Barcelona.

Solution: A sign reading: PUT SOME PANTS ON YOU ARE NOT IN YOUR BATHROOM AT HOME.

Grievance Number 3:

Naked men sawing away at their undercarriages with a towel with one leg placed in an elevated position on a bench. Old men in particular seem to favour this.

Solution: A sign outlawing this action.

Grievance Number 4:

Naked men dressing in the wrong order. First the shirt goes on, then the tie, then the socks, then they sit down and start texting someone, then they rub lotion on their genitals, then they spray themselves with fake tan, then they put their underwear on.

Solution: Pin a series of educational postcards showing the correct sequence for dressing yourself on the changing room walls underneath a sign which simply reads PUT YOUR PANTS ON.

I will now follow this up with a second item named **Gym Weirdo's**.

Here is some other weird behaviour I have personally been affronted by:

<u>The Baby Talk Man:</u> I have regularly heard a man speaking to his sons 'Sammy' and 'Michael' in a baby voice and encouraging them to roar like a lion. Say the words 'Sammy, are you going to roar like a lion?' to yourself in the voice of a five year old and you will get a brief glimpse of how shocking this is. This man's children will grow up entirely lacking resilience. His behaviour is so extreme I have overheard his wife talking in a gruff, masculine timbre – presumably to balance out her wet blanket of a husband. I can only think her two sons are confused. Bizaarely, they both speak to their children using baby voices. I can only imagine they must copulate in an overly aggressive manner to address this imbalance.

<u>The Man Ambling Over To The Scales To Weigh Himself.</u> Then ambling back. Again, naked. No explanation offered or received.

<u>The Men Who Insist On Drying Themselves In The Walkway Between The Showers And Changing Rooms So They Can Admire Themselves In The Mirror.</u>

<u>The Locker Phenomenom:</u> Everytime I go to retrieve my clothes from my locker to get changed, the man with the locker <u>right next to mine</u> comes in to get changed too. Often this is despite the entire rest of the changing room being empty. It's weird. It's a phenomenom. I've noticed it!

<u>The MASSIVE Guy</u> drinking water at the bar with the plastic beaker resembling an egg cup in his giant hand. Could he not bring a bottle of water? I'll answer my own question: this isn't about water, it's about him letting everyone see him and think 'OH MY GOD! THAT GUY IS MASSIVE!! I also observed him stomping up and down the stairs to the CV room with a 40kg dumbbell in each hand. This was not only obstructive to other members, but a health and safety nightmare.

<u>The Bloke Who Knows EVERYONE</u>. He is always in the bar talking to women and he spends more time taking part in gym banter than training. The first time I saw him I somehow KNEW he was divorced. I became involved in a conversation with him and he told me he was an airline pilot but he had to give it up as it didn't pay for the ex-wives. He also claimed to have had £10,000 worth of belongings stolen from his locker. I have no idea what he could have had in his locker that was worth £10,000.

'The Vest' – There is a 65 year old man I have nicknamed 'The Vest.' He wears an old, white P.E. vest and white P.E. shorts. Can he not be guided to dress more appropriately? This is not a 1950's Grammar School gymnasium.

<u>The Utter Dullard:</u> There is a man who talks to many people – in the changing rooms, the spa area and the bar. But all he talks about is the respective temperatures of the jacuzzi and the outdoor pool. He doesn't like it too hot. He can't stand it too cold. It's always too hot or too cold. He is a dullard. Next time I hear him complaining I'm going to say something. The trouble is, he has attracted a faction of wingers who gravitate towards him for a gripe.

In a further worrying development, I appear to have established a number of false friendships. This began when I was conversationally approached by a man in the Jacuzzi who told me without my asking that he had been divorced three times and had a son who had just been awarded a sports scholarship to a top private school. I learned everything from this man except his name and now have to nod a greeting or engage in conversation EVERY SINGLE TIME I see him in the gym.

I DON'T KNOW WHO HE IS!

There is a second man who regularly attends both the gym and Café Sanctuary and seems to have noticed my patronage of both places. He has taken to speaking to me in the gym changing rooms and now mouths 'Good Morning' at me from behind his newspaper whenever I go for a coffee.

I have no idea who he is either.

I like to joke with Rikkesh that I'm being subtly drawn into one big middle class, Guardian reading, West Bridgford Fuck Pie who do weights at the gym and coffee at Café Sanctuary and that *No member of the pie is known by name to other members of the pie. That is the first and only rule of the pie.*

To A Pharmaceutical Company

Thursday 5th February 2009

Dear Sir or Madam,

I am writing to relate my recent experience with one of your products.

I recently came home rather worse for drink and spilt some of your toothpaste on my testicles and penis.

Shortly afterwards my genitals began to burn.

Could you tell me if this is a common experience? I was alarmed by the sensation and wanted to let you know lest any other customers are inadvertently harmed in this way.

Yours Sincerely

Roy Greavesly

Mr Roy Greavesly

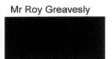

February 03, 2009

Dear Mr Greavesly,

Thank you for your recent letter explaining the problem you have experienced following your use of █████████████████████████

It is possible that people may experience skin irritation from products such as toothpastes if they come into direct contact with skin, particularly more sensitive areas, as you have described. In these circumstances, it is a good general first-aid measure to wash the area thoroughly with large amounts of water.

As an ethical Healthcare Company, it is our policy to document all reactions experienced in connection with our products, and we would therefore be grateful if you would kindly complete the enclosed questionnaire, to provide us with more information about your experience.

If you are still experiencing skin irritation or are in any way concerned, we would recommend that you contact your doctor for further advice.

Thank you for taking the time to contact us and we are sorry for any discomfort you have been caused.

Yours sincerely,

Medical Affairs Department

To A Purveyor Of Citizens Advice

Monday 21st May 2012

Dear Sir or Madam,

I think I may have been initiated into a secret organisation and am writing to ask for your help.

On Friday morning I was in my local coffee shop when a bald headed man nodded at me as he stood up to leave.

I did not know the man and had never seen him before.

Later that afternoon a package arrived for me at work. Inside the package was a small apple pie and a note which read:

The Pie has made contact.

Are you aware of a secret organisation called 'The Pie' operating in the West Bridgford area? I'm unsure of what my next move should be.

Yours sincerely

Roy Greavesly

Mr R Greavesly

Dear Mr Greavesly

Re: Your letter dated 21 May 2012

Thank you for your letter concerning your suspicions about a secret organisation called "The Pie".

"The Pie" is the name of the Notts County fanzine. However we are not aware of any organisation local to West Bridgford which may have contacted you.

It is quite likely that the two events you describe are unrelated. Also the bald man in the coffee shop may have been simply nodding in a general friendly way rather than conveying a message specific to you.

However, if you are concerned, then it might be worth retaining the note you received and listing any behaviour that you regard as unusual just in case you eventually want to talk to a solicitor or even the police.

As the package containing the apple pie was received at your workplace we think you should consider the possibility that it is part of a prank perpetrated by a workmate or workmates.

If you feel upset or disturbed by this event then it could be considered an act of bullying, against which your employer has the responsibility to protect you. You have the option of alerting your line manager to what has happened. We enclose a printout which outlines your employer's responsibilities in this regard, and also how to obtain additional information from ACAS who deal with employment issues.

We trust that this information is useful and helps to clarify your position. However, should you have further queries; you are welcome to contact us again.

Yours sincerely

Deputy Manager

To A Publisher Of Amusing Books

Monday 13th February 2012

Dear Publisher Submissions Team,

I'm writing to submit a collection of letters I've written with the suggestion they be compiled into a highly amusing and profitable book.

The book covers the immediate aftermath of my divorce in 2007 and the madness that followed.

The story of said madness is told by the letters and I must take this opportunity to publicly thank my next door neighbour, Rikkesh, for his support.

Writing these letters is the only thing that has sustained me through my divorce and I will give up writing entirely if you choose not to recognise my talent and publish my book.

I will also move to Norwich entirely against my own will.

I don't know if you've ever been to Norwich, but its road and rail links with the East Midlands are awful. It takes upwards of 3 hours to travel from Nottingham and the locals have no plans for a motorway. They do have an airport but I'm convinced this is for appearances only and that any planes they do have are cardboard models like the Russians had during the Khrushchev era to give the Americans a misleading impression of their military capability.

My ambition is to see my book published and to this end I enclose sample letters from my book and a template for any 'rejection' letter you may try to send me.

Please remember that these are high stakes indeed.

If I receive any letter including the words 'this book is not right for our list' I will quite literally move to Norwich.

I don't want to move to Norwich so please use the letter provided instead.

Finally, I recently read a business book advising me to pen an 'elevator speech,' the idea being that I should be able to sell you on my book idea in the time it takes for us to ride an elevator.

Do you have an elevator at your offices?

If so, please contact me within the next few days to arrange a date and time for me to make my pitch.

I look forward to your letter accepting the cherished mantle of 'publisher' to my utterly brilliant and hilarious book.

I am proud to offer you **The Roy Greavesly Letters**

Yours sincerely

Roy Greavesly

Sample 'Rejection' Letter Template

[../../..]

Dear Roy,

Thank you for your recent submission of **The Roy Greavesly Letters.**

They are hilarious and we want to publish them.

We have published previous collections of letters which were excellent, but have found something different about the humour in yours.

I laughed and laughed when I read that you had hired a helicopter and covered your ex-wife's house in custard!

We simply MUST make you an offer to publish and of course we would be interested to read the sequel.

Come on down to our offices and meet us. We have an elevator and we'd be delighted to hear your pitch.

Yours sincerely

The wonderful team at .... Publishers

Roy Greavesly

Monday 26th March

Dear Mr Greavesly,

Thank you very much for your letter and the enclosed sample material. Whilst it is certainly an interesting idea, unfortunately we have published something very similar before, and are not currently looking to publish another title in this area. Whilst this may come as somewhat disappointing news, we would urge you, however, not to move to Norwich as that 'city' does very little to boost one's self esteem and quality of life. Nottingham has so much more to offer, most notably Ye Olde Trip, Radford and the East Midlands Airport where, I can assure you, they do not use cardboard cut-outs for planes.

Thank you for thinking of ███████████ We do appreciate being given the opportunity to review new material, and would like to wish you every success in finding a home for your idea elsewhere.

Best wishes,

P.S. We do not have an elevator, sadly. We prefer to exercise our older colleagues rigorously with several flights of steep stairs – a sound body makes for a sound mind, after all.

To A Renowned Confectioner

Monday 21st May 2012

Chocolate Bar Helps Greavesly Find Love......

Dear Lovely Customer Relations Team,

In November 2007 I wrote asking if you could fashion a chocolate replica of my head to frighten my recently estranged wife. Karen had left me for a tattooed thirty-two year old electrician and I was not in a good place.

Over the next few years I experienced a meltdown, during which I briefly managed a local band, paraded around a City Centre dressed as Roger Moore, dated a woman called Imogen who was obsessed with Alan Rickman and invited 52 Lord Mayors to participate in an 'Iron Mayor' Contest.

After hiring a friend's helicopter and dumping 60 litres of custard over Karen's new love nest, I realised that things had to change.

At this stage in my story I must ask you to use your powers of visualisation to picture in your head the dramatic scene that follows:

I was in a pub one Friday night when I suddenly realised that Karen had divorced me and that our marriage was in fact over and that I was free. At this very moment the song **'Left To My Own Devices'** by **The Pet Shop Boys** came on.

I must ask you to now play the start of this song so that you can picture what happened next:

I froze in place as my ears caught the first burst of the songs dramatic strings....

My head turned to one side, listening intently like a meerkat...

The disco beat kicked in and I started dancing and once I'd started I was completely unable to stop.

As I danced with abandon I noticed an attractive woman smiling at me.

Later that night a note was pushed through my letterbox.

The note read as follows:

'Hello, I am a very attractive woman and I found your dancing very amusing. You are definitely in with a chance of taking me on a date should you complete the following challenge. During the next week I will be driving around the locality in a bright yellow sports car and I challenge you to find me. Whilst driving I will be singing along to a CD. You must guess the song I am singing, write your answer in a note and leave it in the chip shop. Should you correctly guess the song, you may take me out for dinner at your own expense. Good luck. A very attractive woman.'

Intrigued by the note I decided to play along. The next day I drove around the local area but it was three hours before I caught sight of the yellow sports car and the very attractive woman behind the wheel.

There she was right opposite me at the traffic lights. We made eye contact. She smiled. I scrutinised her features keenly as her lips started to move in tune to the song. After a few seconds I had it! **'JUMP IN MY CAR'** BY **DAVID HASSLEHOFF**

I wrote it down and left my note in the chip shop.

The next day I received my answer when she drove past me and shook her head.

The following day we met again at the traffic lights. She sang a song. I wrote my answer down and left it in the chip shop.

A week later I saw her again. She shook her head. 'This is silly,' I thought and gave chase with some determination. Reaching into the glove compartment I grabbed one of your beautiful chocolate bars and when she stopped at a T junction I ran towards her car and hurled it at her windshield.

She pulled over and got out.

'Well done,' she said. 'You've got my attention. But before you take me out you must pass one more challenge. I'll be in touch.'

Later that night another note came through the letterbox.

'Your taste in chocolate is excellent. I will definitely go out with you if you successfully recreate the pop video: **'Dancing In The Street'** featuring Mick Jagger and David Bowie, outside the pub within the next month and invite everyone to watch.

Shortly after receiving the note I looked up the video on You Tube and can only describe what I saw as an abomination, featuring some of the most appalling hairstyles, clothing and facial expressions I've ever seen.

But I really want to go out with her and feel compelled to do what she says!

Luckily my next door neighbour, Rikkesh, has agreed to be David Bowie, leaving me to portray Mick Jagger, a ludicrous figure at best.

Please immediately watch the video **'Mick Jagger & David Bowie Dancing In The Street'** on YouTube so you can fully appreciate the challenge facing me:

I very much appreciated your kind letter dated 17th December 2007 and do hope you wish me well with my challenge!

I am placing all my hopes for future happiness upon this.

Yours sincerely

Roy Greavesly

31 May 2012

Mr Roy Greavesly

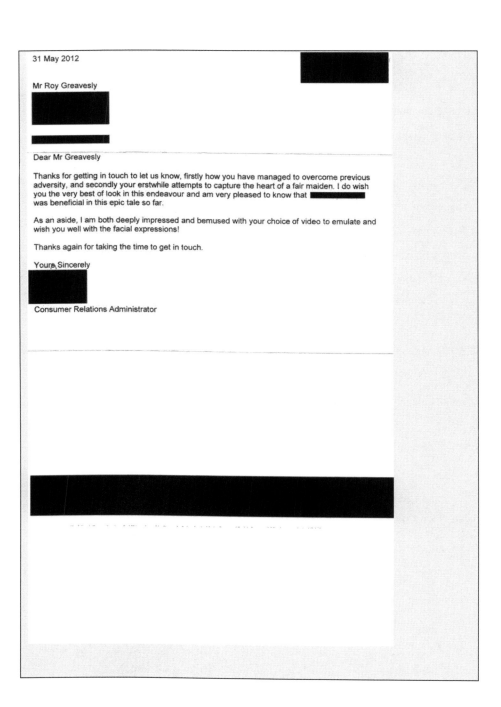

Dear Mr Greavesly

Thanks for getting in touch to let us know, firstly how you have managed to overcome previous adversity, and secondly your erstwhile attempts to capture the heart of a fair maiden. I do wish you the very best of look in this endeavour and am very pleased to know that ███████ was beneficial in this epic tale so far.

As an aside, I am both deeply impressed and bemused with your choice of video to emulate and wish you well with the facial expressions!

Thanks again for taking the time to get in touch.

Yours Sincerely

Consumer Relations Administrator

Who *Is* Roy Greavesly?

Letter writer and sometime dancer, Roy Greavesly is a survivor of divorce, who is now known locally as The Custard Avenger.

Roy Greavesly might also be a pseudonym for Robert Higgs. Robert is a writer of books, plays and films and a comedy writer/performer.

If you've enjoyed this book and would like to read more from its author you can always visit **www.theglisteningtortoise.com** or follow on Twitter @RJHwriter.

'Roy' would be especially keen to read your answers to the following essay question: 'Jump In My Car' by David Hasselhoff. Discuss.'

Printed in Great Britain
by Amazon.co.uk, Ltd.,
Marston Gate.